Lugano
Switzerland

City Map

 Glob:us

Lugano, Switzerland — City Map
By Jason Patrick Bates

First Edition: February 2017

Scale / 1:4000

50m

500ft

Map Overview

Map Symbols

Highway		Map continuation page	
Street		Path	
Archaeological site		Kiosk	
Artwork		Level crossing	
Atm		Library	
Bar		Lighthouse	
Bicycle rental		Memorial	
Biergarten		Memorial plaque	
Buddhist temple		Monument	
Bus station		Museum	
Bus stop		Muslim mosque	
Cafe		Neighbourhood	
Camping site		Nightclub	
Car rental		Parking	
Cave entrance		Peak	
Chalet		Pharmacy	
Charging station		Picnic site	
Church / Monastery		Playground	
Cinema		Police	
Courthouse		Post office	
Department store		Prison	
Dog park		Pub	
Drinking water		Railway	
Dry cleaning		Restaurant	
Elevator		Shinto temple	
Embassy		Sikh temple	
Fast food		Sports centre	
Ferry terminal		Supermarket	
Fire station		Taoist temple	
Fountain		Taxi	
Fuel		Telephone	
Golf course		Theatre	
Guest house		Toilets	
Hindu temple		Townhall	
Hospital		Traffic signals	
Hostel		Viewpoint	
Hotel		Water park	
Information		Wilderness hut	
Jewish synagogue		Windmill	

Via del Sole

Via del Sole

Via Vedo

Via Miralago

Via Miralago

Via Giuseppe Guioni

Strada di Pregassona

Salita Viarno

Salita Viarno

Via Crocetta

Via Pazzalino

Via Max Frisch

Via Sara

17

6

Via Zurigo

Via Losanna

Via Soldati

Via Vincenzo Vanoni

Via Trevano

P

Via Antonio Vanoni

P

Via Vincenzo Vanoni

Via Carlo M

Via Antonio Ciseri

Via Generale Dufour

Via Zurigo

Via Berna

Viale Stefano Franscini

Via Giuseppe Curti

Via Carlo Maderno

Via Ferruccio Pelli

Parco Villa Saroli

Via D'Alberti

Via D'Alberti

Via Greina

P

Via Generale Dufour

Via Ginevra

Via Serafino Balestra

Via Ferruccio Pelli

P

Via Alberto Giacometti

Via Pretorio

Via E. Bossi

tista Ploda

27
Gendarmeria

Via La Santa

Via Bottogno

Via la Santa

Mappa del comune di Lugano

la Santa

Via alla Chiesa

Via Muggina

Via agli Orti

Via al Lido

Via alla Roggia

Via della Pergola

Via alla Chiesa

Via Molinazzo

Via al Chioso

Via delle Scuole

Via Maggio

Viale dei Faggi

Via Maggio

Via del Tiglio

Via del Tiglio

Via delle Scuole

Via Campo Marzio

Via Concordia

Viale dei Faggi

8

29

Via San Nicolao

Via Pontaccio

Via Ruviana

Via Roccolo

Albonago

Via S. navista

Juvigliana

Via Aldesago

31

Sentiero Cureggia

Utoring

Via Aldesago

Via Barè

Via Barè

Via Bassone

Via Rava

Caregott

Via Aldesago

Sen... o Buz

32

Monte Brè

Via Vetta

Via Brè

33

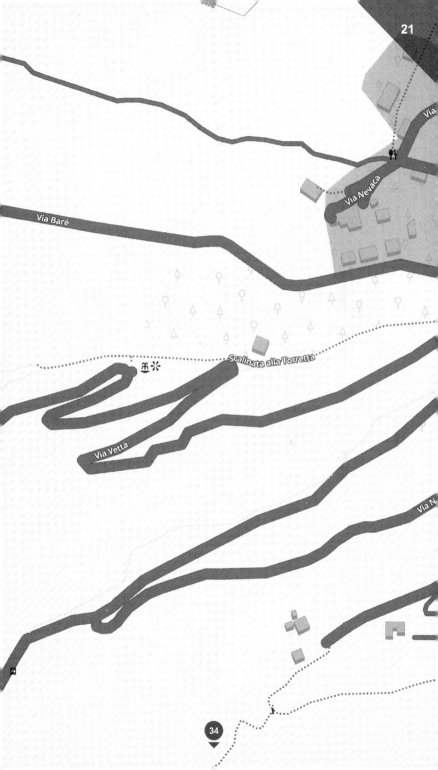

Via

Via Nevaca

Via Baré

Scalinata alla Torretta

Via Vetta

Via N

34

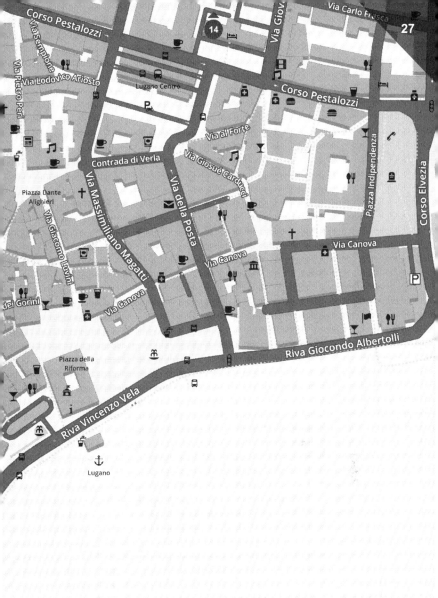

Corso Pestalozzi

Via Sempione

Via Lodovico Ariosto

Via Pietro Peri

Lugano Centro

Corso Pestalozzi

Via al Forte

Contrada di Verla

Via Giosuè Carducci

Piazza Indipendenza

Corso Elvezia

Via Massimiliano Magatti

Via della Posta

Piazza Dante Alighieri

Via Giacomo Luvini

Via Canova

Via Canova

Via Canova

dei Gorini

Riva Giocondo Albertolli

Piazza della Riforma

Riva Vincenzo Vela

Lugano

fondazione
Filippo Ciani

Viale Carlo Cattaneo

Via Pasquale Lu

uigi Lavizzari

Via Landri

Capelli

15

Viale Carlo Cattaneo

Piazza Castello

Palazzo Congressi
Lugano

Villa Ciani

Tennis

Parco Civico
Villa Ciani

Biblioteca
Cantonale
di Lugano

Museum
natural Lugano

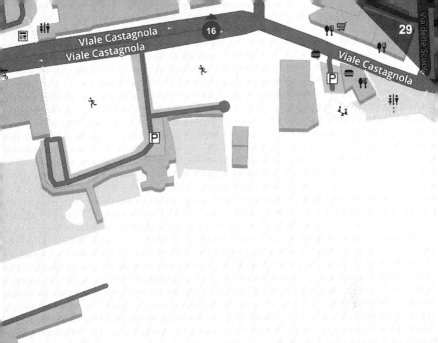

Viale Castagnola
Viale Castagnola

16

Viale Castagnola

Start 7

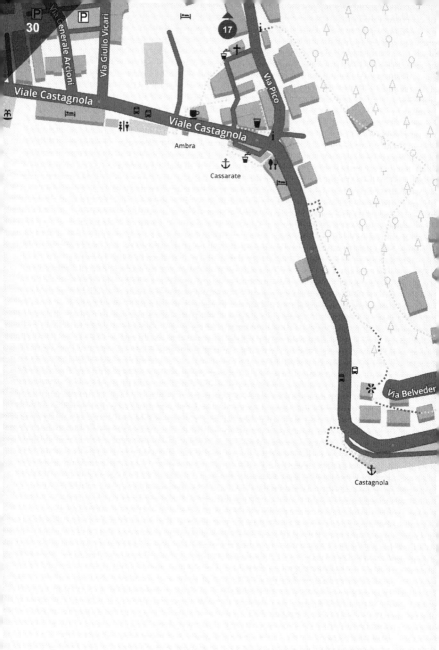

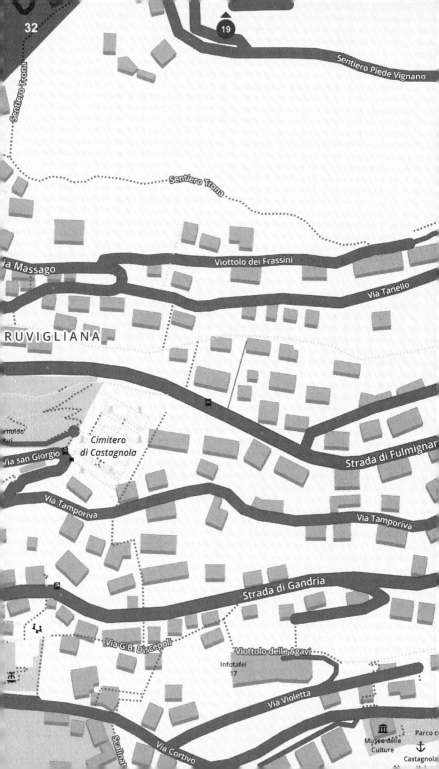

Via Vall'Orba

Stra

Oliveto
Sperimentale

Parco dell'Olivo

Infotafel

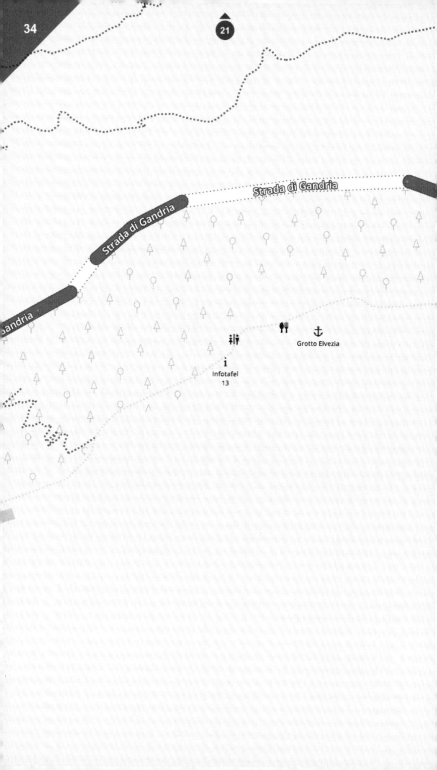

21

Strada di Gandria

Strada di Gandria

Gandria

Grotto Elvezia

Infotafel
13

23

Roggia di Cremignone

Via

Ponte Tresa

41

chetto

Paradiso

e Cattori

Riva Paradiso

Via San Salvatore

Via General Guisan

Via Gerretta

Via delle Scuole

Via Ernesto Bosia

P

Via ai Grotti

Paradiso

Via Carona

Via Carona

Via Guidino

Parco Guidino

Streets

C

Contrada dei patrizi . . . 9
Contrada di sassello . 26, 27
Contrada di verla 27
Contrada vecchio municipio 31
Corsia autobus 39
Corso elvezia . . 14, 15, 27
Corso enrico pestalozzi 27
Corso pestalozzi 27
Crocicchio cortogna . 27
Cà di sotto 41

G

Galleria collina d'oro 40, 41
Gradinata albonago . . 17, 18
Gradinata can. angiolo pimetta 12
Gradinata dafne . . 13, 26
Gradinata della bressanella 39
Gradinata della valle . 18
Gradinata delle rose . 39
Gradinata massena 5, 13
Gradinata mimosa . . . 26
Gradinata pometta . . . 12
Gradinata vincenzo arnaboldi 26

P

Pedonale nolci 12
Piazza alessandro manzoni 27
Piazza bernardino luini 39

Piazza carlo battaglini 26
Piazza carlo cattaneo 31
Piazza castello 27, 28
Piazza cioccaro 26
Piazza dante alighieri 27
Piazza della riforma . . 27
Piazza della riscossa 29, 30
Piazza emilio bossi . . . 30
Piazza indipendenza . 27
Piazza molino nuovo . 14, 15
Piazza riforma 27
Piazza riziero rezzonico 27
Piazza san giorgio 31
Piazza stefano franscini 30
Piazzale della stazione 26
Piazzale di besso . 25, 26
Piazzale stazione 26
Piazzetta emilio maraini 27
Piazzetta san carlo . . . 26
Piazzetta san rocco . . 27

R

Riva antonio caccia . . 39, 44
Riva giocondo albertolli 27
Riva paradiso 44, 45
Riva vincenzo vela . . . 26, 27, 39

S

Salita alla chiesa 31
Salita carlo bossoli . . . 26
Salita degli angioli . . . 39

Salita degli olivi 31
Salita dei castagni 31
Salita dei frati 13
Salita dei narcissi 32
Salita delle ginestre . . 17
Salita di vallèe 30, 31
Salita don g. storni . . . 22
Salita mario e antonio chiattone 26, 27
Salita san grato 33
Salita viarno 8, 9
Scalinata alla torretta . 21
Scalinata dei sassi . . . 32
Scalinata della torretta 20
Scalinata jose belloni 38, 39
Scalinata nicolò laghi 14
Scalinata oleandri 32
Scorciatoia 6
Sentiero al pizzo . . 19, 20
Sentiero baregott . 18, 19
Sentiero boggiogna . 30, 31
Sentiero buzzanello . 19, 32
Sentiero campaccio . 18, 19
Sentiero campagna . . 31, 32
Sentiero camporago . . 3
Sentiero cureggia . . . 19
Sentiero delle betulle 20, 21
Sentiero di gandria . . 33, 34
Sentiero piede vigano 21
Sentiero piede vignano 32, 33
Sentiero roncaretto . . 10
Sentiero trona . 19, 31–33
sotto ceneri nationale autostrada 41

Strada bagion 41
Strada cantonale 40
Strada da pambi 42
Strada dal brügon 42
Strada dal cioss . . . 41, 42
Strada dal mator· 42
Strada dal ort 42
Strada di fulmignano
    31–33
Strada di gandria . 31–34
Strada di noch 42
Strada di pregassona . 9
Strada gesora 41, 42
Strada regina 38, 39
Strada sapèll 42
Strecia dal torc . . . 41, 42

V

Via adamina 10, 23
Via adolfo e oscar torri-
    celli 6
Via agli orti 16
Via ai canvetti 40
Via ai grotti 36, 41, 44
Via ai lotti 3
Via ai ronchi 23
Via al boschetto 43
Via al bosco 5
Via al campanile 9
Via al chioso 15, 16
Via al colle . 12, 25, 37, 38
Via al cottorado 41
Via al fiume 8
Via al forte 27
Via al laghetto 24, 36, 37
Via al lido 16
Via al municipio 13
Via al nido 12
Via al perato 22
Via al ponte 12, 13
Via al roccolo 10
Via al ruscello 17, 18
Via al sapel 42
Via al sapell 41
Via al teglio 35
Via al tiglio 16
Via albano 11, 12
Via alberto giacometti 14
Via albonago . . . 9, 17, 18
Via aldesago . . 18, 19, 31,
    32
Via alessandro volta . . 15
Via alla campagna . 7, 24
Via alla chiesa 16
Via alla chiesa di biogno
    22

Via alla foce 28, 29
Via alla fontana 31
Via alla roggia 16, 17
Via alla selva 35
Via alla valletta . . . 38, 43
Via alle caragne 6, 7
Via alle cave 41
Via alle dobbie . . 24, 37
Via alle fontane 41
Via alle vigne 24
Via alta 41
Via antonio adamini . 38,
    39
Via antonio barzaghi . 44
Via antonio ciseri 14
Via antonio fogazzaro 15
Via antonio fusoni 15
Via antonio galli . . 13, 26
Via antonio riva 38
Via antonio vanoni . . . 14
Via aprica 25, 26
Via avv. b. leoni . . 10, 22,
    23, 35
Via baldassare
    longhena 6
Via baroffio 13, 26
Via baré 19–21
Via basilea 13, 26
Via bassone 19
Via battista foletti 12
Via bellavista 17, 18
Via beltramina 7, 8
Via belvedere . . 4, 30, 31,
    37
Via berenice 41, 42
Via berna 14
Via bernardino stazio . 13
Via bertaccio 26
Via bertaro lam-
    bertenghi 15
Via besso 3, 11, 12, 25, 26
Via bioggio 3
Via bolio 10, 22
Via bonoli 10, 11, 23
Via bora da besa . 40, 41
Via boschina 8
Via boscioro 7, 8, 15
Via bottogno . . . 9, 16, 17
Via breganzona . . . 11, 12
Via brenno bertoni 24, 25
Via brentino 43
Via bré 19–21, 33
Via c. a. bernasconi . . 13
Via ca' di sopra 41
Via cabione 4, 12
Via calprino 43
Via camara 3, 10

Via camoghè 15
Via campagna 4, 40
Via campagna di bre-
    ganzona 10,
    11
Via campagne 40
Via campo dei fiori . . 3, 4
Via campo marzio 15, 16
Via campo sportivo . 3, 4
Via canevali 27
Via canonica 15
Via canova 27
Via cantonale 4, 9, 13, 14,
    27
Via canva 4
Via capelli 15, 28
Via cara 22
Via carlo frasca 27
Via carlo maderno . . . 14
Via carlo martignoni 3, 4
Via carolina maraini-
    sommaruga 6
Via carona 43, 44
Via carzo 43
Via casarico 23
Via cassarinetta 43
Via castagnola 30
Via castausio 6, 14
Via castelletto 37
Via cattedrale 26
Via caustasio 6
Via ceresio . . 8, 12, 17, 18,
    31
Via cesare cantù 6
Via chioso 41, 42
Via ciani 7
Via ciusarella 3, 4
Via ciusaretta 35
Via clemente maraini 13,
    26, 38, 39
Via colle 37
Via collina 9, 17
Via collina d'oro . 38, 40,
    43
Via concordia 16, 17
Via contrada vecchia 24
Via coremmo . . 12, 13, 25
Via cortivallo 12, 24
Via cortivo 31–33
Via costera 10
Via cremignone . . 23, 24
Via crevuglio 10
Via crocetta 8, 9
Via crocietta 9
Via cà di sopra 41, 42
Via d'alberti 14
Via degli albrizzi 27

Via degli amadio 26
Via degli oliva 26, 27
Via dei bonoli 10
Via dei casagrande . . 10
Via dei castagna . . 26, 27
Via dei fiori 37
Via dei gelsi 8, 9
Via dei gorini 27
Via dei panora 22
Via dei pesci 27
Via dei pioppi 11, 12
Via dei platani 4, 12
Via dei portici 35
Via dei ronchi 6
Via dei sindicatori 12
Via dei solari 26, 27
Via del bosco 18, 19
Via del canvetto 6, 7
Via del pozzo 8, 10
Via del sole 8, 9
Via del tiglio 15–17
Via della pergola 16
Via della posta 27
Via della salute 31
Via delle aie 7
Via delle primule 31
Via delle rose 8
Via delle scuole 4, 12, 16,
   29, 43, 44
Via delle vigne 31–33
Via dogana vecchia . 26,
   27
Via domenico fontana
   39, 43, 44
Via don giuseppe
   gagliardi 22, 23
Via dott. giov. polar . . 10,
   11, 23
Via e. bossi 14
Via emilio maraini . . . 4, 5
Via ernesto bosia 44
Via ernesto pelloni 7
Via eugenio montale . 9,
   17
Via ferruccio pelli 14
Via foce 29
Via fola 8
Via fontanella 22
Via formellino 36, 37
Via francesco borromini
   25, 26
Via francesco mola 7
Via francesco petrarca
   27
Via francesco soave . 26,
   27

Via francesco somani 14,
   15
Via franco zorzi . . . 43, 44
Via funicolare 30
Via fusoni 15
Via g. b. discepoli . 31, 32
Via g. canevascini . 11, 12
Via g.b. discepoli . 31, 32
Via g.b. dominione 15, 16
Via gaggini da bissone
   38, 39
Via gemmo 11, 24
Via general guisan . 8, 9,
   44
Via generale arcioni . . 30
Via generale dufour . . 14
Via generale h. guisan 3,
   4, 11
Via generoso 38
Via genzana 12, 13
Via gerolamo vegezzi 27
Via gerretta 44
Via gerso 13
Via giacomo brentani . 7,
   8
Via giacomo e filippo
   ciani 7, 8, 15
Via giacomo luvini . . . 27
Via giacomo mercoli 6, 7
Via gian giacomo
   rosseau 25, 26
Via ginevra 14
Via giosué carducci . . 27
Via giovan battista pi-
   oda 14,
   27
Via giovanni ferri 6, 7
Via giovanni nizzola . . 27
Via giovanni serodine 12
Via giroggio 37, 38
Via giuglielmo marconi
   27
Via giulio pocobelli . . 26
Via giulio vicari 17, 30
Via giuseppe bagutti . 7,
   14, 15
Via giuseppe buffi . 14, 15
Via giuseppe cattori . 43,
   44
Via giuseppe curti 14, 15
Via giuseppe guioni . . . 9
Via giuseppe lepori 4, 11
Via giuseppe mazzini 38,
   39
Via giuseppe motta . . . 4,
   12, 13, 26, 39
Via giuseppe parini . . . 15

Via giuseppe petrini 6, 7
Via giuseppe stabile . 25,
   26
Via giuseppe zoppi . . . 13
Via greina 14, 15
Via guggirolo 17
Via guglielmo marconi
   27
Via guidino 44, 45
Via guido calgari 43
Via henri durant 11
Via in selva 22
Via ing. luigi casale . . 22,
   23
Via la roggia 24
Via la santa 15, 16
Via laghetto 36, 40
Via landriani 15, 28
Via lema 12, 13
Via lisano 12
Via lodovico ariosto . . 27
Via loreto 38, 39
Via losanna 6, 14
Via lucerna 13, 25
Via luciano zuccoli . . . 43
Via lucino 10, 11, 23
Via ludovico ariosto . . 27
Via luganetto 15, 16
Via lugano 24, 25
Via luigi canonica . 14, 15
Via luigi lavizzari . . 15, 28
Via luigi taddei 8, 16
Via lurati 15
Via m. d. carona 7, 15
Via madonetta 14, 15
Via madonna della
   salute 11–13
Via madonnetta 15
Via maggio 15–17
Via maolino 22
Via maraini 5
Via maraini sommaruga
   6
Via marco da carona . . 7,
   15
Via marconi 27
Via massagno 13
Via massago 31, 32
Via massimiliano maga-
   tti 27
Via mattro 3
Via max frisch 9
Via medi 10
Via merlina 8, 16
Via miralago 9
Via miralago di castag-
   nola 32

Via molinazzo 16, 17
Via moncucchetto . . . 24
Via moncucco 24, 25
Via mons. angelo
    jelmini 12, 25
Via montalbano . . 38, 42,
    43
Via montarina 26
Via montarinetta 26
Via monte boglia 7, 8
Via monte bre 7, 15
Via monte brè 15
Via monte carmen . 6, 14
Via morella 4
Via morena 11
Via moretto 23, 24
Via muggina 16, 17
Via muzzano . . 23, 35, 36
Via nassa 26, 27, 39
Via nava 22
Via navone 4, 5
Via nevaca 21
Via noale 38
Via nocc 42
Via nolgio 12
Via nonato 21
Via nosedo 11, 12
Via orbisana 22
Via orti 15
Via oscar e adolfo torri-
    celli 6
Via panera 37, 38
Via paolo regazzoni . . 13,
    26
Via pasquale lucchini 15,
    28
Via pasquee 12
Via pazzalino 9, 16
Via pedemonte 9, 17
Via perato 22
Via peri 27
Via pessina 26, 27
Via piazza indipendenza
    27
Via pico 17, 30
Via pietro peri 27
Via pietro solaro . . . 5, 13
Via pontaccio 18
Via ponte tresa 25,
    36-38, 40, 41
Via povrò 3, 4
Via praccio 4, 5
Via prada 23, 24
Via pradello 10
Via pretorio 14, 27

Via privata maraini . . 5, 6
Via quiete 38, 39
Via r. manzoni 13
Via rava 8, 16, 19
Via restabbio 41
Via ricordone 6
Via righetto 37
Via rinaldo siemen 7
Via rinaldo simen . . 7, 15
Via rino tami 24, 37
Via risciana 40, 41
Via riviera 30-32
Via roccolo 18
Via rodari 26
Via romeo manzoni . . 13,
    26
Via roncaccio 25
Via ronchetto 6, 7, 36, 41,
    42
Via rossago 22
Via rovello 5
Via rovencano 35
Via rovere 11
Via rubiana 41, 42
Via ruggero dollfus von
    volkersberg 31
Via ruviana 18
Via ruvigliana 9, 17
Via san carlo 3, 11
Via san giorgio 31, 32
Via san gottardo . 3-5, 13
Via san grato 37
Via san lorenzo 26
Via san michele 31
Via san nicolao 18
Via san pietro pambio 43
Via san salvatore . . 5, 13,
    44
Via sant'abbondio . . . 37,
    40-42
Via sara frontini . . . 9, 17
Via sarera 22
Via sass curona 22
Via sassa 5, 6
Via selva 5, 13, 24
Via sempione 27
Via serafino balestra . 14,
    15
Via serenella 31
Via sguancia 43
Via silvio calloni . . 38, 43
Via sione 5, 13
Via sione;via solaro 5
Via solaro 13
Via soldati 6, 13, 14

Via soldino 11, 12, 25
Via sole 4
Via somazzi 22, 23
Via sorengo . . . 11, 25, 26
Via sorgente 19
Via sotto sala 9
Via speranza 15, 16
Via stauffacher 27
Via stefano franscini . . 14
Via tamporiva 32, 33
Via tanello 32, 33
Via tassino 25, 26, 38, 39
Via tervano 14
Via tesserete 5, 6, 13
Via tomaso rodari 25, 26
Via torquato tasso . . . 26
Via torricelli 6
Via trevano 6, 7, 14
Via ugo foscolo 39
Via val gersa 4
Via vall'orba 32, 33
Via valleggia 23, 24
Via vedo 9
Via vergiò 10, 11
Via vetta 20, 21
Via vignola 7
Via vincenzo vanoni . . 14
Via violetta 32
Via vira 5
Via visano 22, 23, 35
Via vittorino vella 17
Via zurigo 13-15
Viale battista foletti 4, 12
Viale carlo cattaneo . 27,
    28
Viale cassarate . . . 15, 28
Viale castagnola . 28-30
Viale dei faggi 16, 29
Viale stefano franscini 14
Vicolo chioso 23
Vicolo cisterna 23, 24, 37
Vicolo dei conti . . 10, 23
Vicolo dei pini 9
Vicolo del grano . . 26, 27
Vicolo del lido 27
Vicolo nassetta 26
Vicolo orfanotrofio . . . 27
Vicolo soldini-condy . 13
Vicolo vecchio 13
Viottlolo dei frassini . . 32
Viottolo centrale 31
Viottolo dei frassini . . . 32
Viottolo delle agavi . . 32,
    33

Points of Interest

B

Bus Station 🚌 27

C

Canton Police-
    Gardermeria (Bossi
    2) 🚓 14
Casa Pasquée Events
    Hall 🏛 12
Castagnola 🏢 31
Cathedral San Lorenzo
    and View Point
    over the City 👤 . . 26
Chapel Maria Assunta
    👤 20
Chapel San Pietro Er-
    bette 👤 30
Church Sacro Cuore
    (G.Maderno 20) 👤
    14
Church San Antonio
    Abate (Piazza
    A.Dante) 👤 27
Church San Carlo
    (Nassa 22) 👤 . . . 26
Church San Giorgio 👤 31
Church San Gotardo 👤
    13
Church Santa Lucia 👤 12
Church Santa Maria As-
    sunta 👤 37
Church Santa Maria
    degli Angioli 👤 . . 39
Church Santa Maria Im-
    macolata (P.Peri 9)
    👤 27
Church Santa Teresa 👤
    16
Church Sts.Quirico and
    Giullita 👤 22

Ciani Villa-Events Hall
    👤 28
Clinic Moncucco ✚ . . 25
Clinic San Rocco ✚ . . . 11
Commune di Lugano-
    Town Hall 👤 27
Congress Palace 👤 . . 28

F

Ferry Terminal Cas-
    sarate ⚓ 30
Ferry Terminal Castag-
    nola ⚓ 30
Ferry Terminal Grotto
    Elvezia ⚓ 34
Ferry Terminal Museo
    Heleneum ⚓ 32
Ferry Terminal Paradiso
    ⚓ 44
Foundation Filippo Ciani
    🏛 28
Funicular Station Al-
    bonago 🚞 18
Funicular Station Alde-
    sago 🚞 19
Funicular Station Bré-
    Villaggio 🚞 20
Funicular Station Cas-
    sarate 🚞 30
Funicular Station Città
    🚞 26
Funicular Station Monte
    Bré 🚞 20
Funicular Station
    Stazione 🚞 26
Funicular Station Su-
    vigliana 🚞 18
Funicular Station Utor-
    ing 🚞 19

H

Hospital Italiano ✚ . . . 15
Hospital Regional ✚ . . 6
Hospital Sant'Anna ✚ 37,
    38

I

Italo-Swiis University-
    USI 🏛 15

L

LAC-Museum of Italo-
    Swiss Art 🏛 39
Lake Muzzano 👤 . 35, 36
Lugano Casino (Canova
    and Stauffacher 1)
    👤 27
Lugano Central Ferry
    Terminal ⚓ 27

M

Municipality of Mas-
    sagno 👤 13
Museum Erba-
    Children's Museum
    (R.Caccia 1) 🏛 . . . 39
Museum of Art Anna
    Braglia 🏛 39
Museum of Culture-
    Villa Heleneum 🏛
    32
Museum of Italo-Swiss
    Art (Canova 10) 🏛
    27
Museum of Natural His-
    tory 🏛 28
Music Conservatory 🏛
    25
Muzzano 🏢 35

Printed in Poland
by Amazon Fulfillment
Poland Sp. z o.o., Wrocław